"BY THIS TIME"

poems by

Ian Ganassi

Finishing Line Press
Georgetown, Kentucky

"BY THIS TIME"

Copyright © 2024 by Ian Ganassi
ISBN 979-8-88838-475-6 First Edition
All rights reserved under International and Pan-American Copyright Conventions. No part of this book may be reproduced in any manner whatsoever without written permission from the publisher, except in the case of brief quotations embodied in critical articles and reviews.

Publisher: Leah Huete de Maines
Editor: Christen Kincaid
Cover Art: "Discipline" by Laura Bell and Ian Ganassi
Author Photo: David Ganassi
Cover Design: Elizabeth Maines McCleavy

Order online: www.finishinglinepress.com
also available on amazon.com

Author inquiries and mail orders:
Finishing Line Press
PO Box 1626
Georgetown, Kentucky 40324
USA

Contents

The Other Hand 1
The Apples 2
The Usual Miscalculations 4
"By This Time" 5
Fancy-Dress Ball 7
Offerings 8
Helicon 9
Ambient Emergencies 10
Board Meeting 11
Keeping Busy 12
Whatever Works 13
Mandatory Compulsion 14
Woolly Mammoth 15
Where is "Away?" 16
Trap Door 17
Utility Belt 18
Hazy on the Details 19
Catchy Tune 21
Feasibility Study 22
Manufacturing Sector 24
Reunion 25
Dead Blues 26
Unspoken Regulations 28
A Flaw of Wind 29
A Steady and Sinister Serenity 30
In Her Dream 31
Current Conditions 33
Is This a Test? 34
Crawling Around 35
Strange Brew 36
Fluid Situation 38

Silver Bullet	39
Wandering Down	40
A Feather in your Skull	41
False Pretenses	42
Rubbernecking	43
Hot Tamales	44
Wheel of Fortune	45
Water Water	47
Undeniably	48
March Time	49
Static Silence	50
Free-Floating Anxiety	51
Does a Bear?	52
Striptease	53
True North	54
Responsory	55
Twenty Mules	56
White Noise	57
Aggressive Ingrates	58
The Incredible Shrinking Man	59
Stupid Question	61
Chance Encounter	62
Accidental Disaster	63
The Apple of Discord	64
High Noon	66
The Birds	68
Study Group	70
Waiting Room	71
Haunting and Hunting	73
General Drift	75
ACKNOWLEDGMENTS	77

To my Sister Jill

The real poetry is beyond us, beyond them ...
—Jack Spicer

THE OTHER HAND

The triathlon only lasts until we die.

It was a strange story.

The endings we can no longer bear to look into.

The bridge of sighs,

The fountain of tears,

The bottomless pit of sleep.

He vomited forth the butterflies that were plaguing his stomach. Someone said it was "magical realism."

It "'becomes' a catch-22."

Blues figures on a harmonica.

"Don't worry, you won't get addicted."

"Thanks, Ralph."

Painted figures and written figures.

Strange figures, weird figures.

It all figures. Seven figures.
You figure, we figure, I figure, go figure.
Plaster or porcelain figures,

My father's grace on the ice,

And so on and so forth.

"I would avoid the plural."

What good advice.

THE APPLES

Like dessert,
There was always room for embarrassment.

He was made to work the land, and he hated it,

And formal dinners on Sunday.

Sophisticated in worldly things,
Contemptuous of those who aren't,

One false move and you're in exile.

I was comfortable for a while,
But so much intervened along the way.

And the boys they like to be mean.

There's a storm coming in, batten the hatches.

The feral cat bolted.

These were methods of communication,
His face intent on the blackberries
Between the weeds.

At least we won't have to wade through the shambles.

Not to mention swim through them.

As per usual, she liked "regular" things.
Or things she took to be "regular"—
"Regular guys," for instance.

She thought he was, but he wasn't.
He thought he was, but he wasn't.

Humming an approximation of a show tune,
He liked the sound of his own scat.

The bicycle repairman was full of information—
The wrong kind of information.

So much for a day in country.

THE USUAL MISCALCULATIONS

Like trying to plug the holes in a sieve,

It could have been worse, but not by much.

A bowling buddy?
A driver of last resort?

"Home, Hives!"
"Unsend, Unsend," "Abort, Abort."
We have wasted our lives.

Sam the Sham and the Pharaohs
Were an indelible part of the show.

The color of their roots were on display.

I guess you're as much you as you can be.
So am I, but we're playing in different keys.

"I don't know what I'm going to play," he repeated.

Egrets from the train window.
(Not to mention regrets.)

It is posed and it is posed,
What in nature merely grows.

"Ah, good taste! What a dreadful thing!"

Blue moon, blue cheese,
And whatever else she wanted to sing.

Funny how I didn't see that coming. I did see it going however.
The executioner took his time as he fondled the lever.

Taking a long time to come to bad decisions:
At the hanging the criminal's head popped off
Due to someone's miscalculation.

"BY THIS TIME"

"Frequent streets are another key part
In the physical and social construction of cities."

What's left of the wilderness is no analgesic,

Though there's more of it
Than you might think.

For instance it's surprising
That there's anything left to burn
In California.

White picket fences burning on your lawn,
By this time.

She lived in the exurbs
By this time.
She had a big garden.
She was cooking prime rib.
It was fall.

A runder of thumble could be heard on the gramophone.

The sheriff doesn't like it.
Don't twist his arm.

I subjected myself to the juke box
In another life.

And "Sympathy for the Devil."
I have none.

"You mean that little 'starter' house?"

I'd like to brand you with the OK Corral.

The fires indicate the end of time.
By this time.

But the fiddler pays no attention,
And continues playing
Bonaparte's Retreat or Turkey in the Straw,
Interminably.

As long as the fiddler keeps fiddling
The world will not end.

But who believes
That sort of thing
By this time,

When everyone
Has a mortgage?

By this time.

FANCY-DRESS BALL

I am baffled by the search terms and engines.

I'm baffled by the raffle.

And the rattle.

Don't break the glass, this is only a test.
The news is what will keep you abreast.

The shoemaker is still
Around, here and there,
Like the Goodyear Blimp
Or the guy who sharpens
Knives from his truck.

And speaking of the old days,

Hugh Hefner was an avatar of sorts,
In good ways and bad.

"We were looking at the same book."
"Maybe the book scared him."

Eventually, you too might found an institution.
As for your visit to the reception area, please try your call later.

Purple weather is all the rage.

And the purple grapes in the vineyards
Are suffering the weather with the rest of us.

Whose cabbage is on the block now?

The bank guard began covetous but soon grew bored,
Like a museum attendant with esthetic aspirations.

Once you hear the details of victory, it is hard to distinguish from defeat.

The rag-ends of our coats and other dilapidated paraphernalia.
Don't look now, but I think it's time to put the costumes away.

OFFERINGS

Accused of a crime I was considered to have considered,
I preferred to stay in bed.

"You've beaten and you've been beaten"
Was the theme of *The Lost Weekend*.

Me no like.

The thought or speech balloon
Gets halfway there and then deflates.

The anonymity of glamour, the glamour of anonymity,
Dark glasses in the middle of the night.

I've about had it.

It depends at what depth one focuses the lens,
At what power of magnification.

Shocking where he got off,
On the train platform in what seemed
The middle of nowhere.

I'd like to buy the world a Coke.

I'll have to have one with my broker.

All the various offerings are worth a hill of beans.

The best defense against germs is to ignore them.

She had a vivid orange in her tortoise shell pattern.

My paraphrase can't compete with the original.

Prestidigitation, misdirection,
Valentine cards and mourning doves ...

But no satisfying explanation of the snake
That crawled out of Anchises's tomb.

HELICON

The smart set was high on a diet of worms.
        The teacher said it was a book you have to study,
But maybe I wasn't interested in writing that way.
        With all the confusion the fountain gets muddy.

The cemetery closes promptly at 4:30 p.m.
        Don't get locked in with the cold.
Death is a friendly/friendless sort of dilemma,
        Especially when it's time to get old.

It's not just a song, it's a song with an overture.
        He said it was a book you have to study.
And don't call me Rover, I'm not your little dog.
        With all the confusion the fountain got muddy.

The girl with kaleidoscope eyes ...
        Don't get locked in with the cold.
"The girl with colitis goes by."
        Especially when it's time to get old.

Someone came to the rescue but nobody paid the rent.
        He said it was a book you have to study.
Poverty really does suck; I can't afford to go on.
        With all the confusion the fountain got muddy.

Sometimes we would go to the dump and find a lot of filth.
        Don't get locked in with the cold—
There's no such thing as "valuable" junk,
        Even when it's time to get old.

We were barbarians with a yawp.
        The teacher said it was a book you have to study.
You need more than love and imagination.
        With all the confusion the fountain gets muddy.

"Poets know from being bums," she said.
        Don't get locked in with the cold—
Loneliness is a kind of freedom
        Even when it's time to get old.

AMBIENT EMERGENCIES

Whichever way the sign points, go the other way.
The kid upstairs likes to hear herself scream.
He left a suicide note that said he really wanted to stay.

Calm evenings are the exception, it's easier during the day.
Why does the kid upstairs like to hear herself scream?
Whichever way the sign points, go the other way.

No amount of figuring will tell you why she sounds that way.
Whatever your conjecture, it's not the way it seems.
He left a suicide note that said he really wanted to stay.

I spend more time than I should ciphering the neighbors' games.
It isn't who or what you know it's who or what you've seen.
Whichever way the sign points, go the other way.

I'm only speculating here, don't look at me that way.
Since the grass is dead on my side, over there it must be green.
He left a suicide note that said he really wanted to stay.

I know exactly what you mean but I'd rather not say.
You'll never get ahead at that rate of speed.
But whichever way the sign points, go the other way.
He left a suicide note that said he really wanted to stay.

BOARD MEETING

The handyman was painting the room.
It was enough to calculate, but not enough to matter.
He knew we were coming and got out the broom.

They slaughtered the fatted steer. It was a party.
Sentimental claptrap like curtains hung in a manhole—
There was no shortage. They called him "shorty"

Because he was seven feet tall. Anger and madness
Must be subsumed. Otherwise, who will herd the cattle?
Who will paint the room? Who will play with the rattle?

No more questions if you don't have answers.
There's no charge for the apple pie,
Let's hope it doesn't give you cancer.

In the news, they put a man on the moon.
Turns out it's made of cheese after all.
It's very good cheese, if you have the right spoon,

And better than Tang and other "astronaut food."
Table the minutes and ignore the baboons,
The bell is going to ring in a second anyhow.

Just get up early to enjoy the cartoons.
It was time to break out in the usual acne.
Unfortunately, the Oldsmobile was running on fumes.

Friends of the deceased are invited to the event:
The piper crooning all the little piggies to market;
The grasshoppers in the manhole growing darker.

KEEPING BUSY

The hardware store clerk had a hobby:
Drinking all night, he assembled
Model trains. His hobby, however, was drinking.

"I'm getting out of this business," he said.

Thank God for Social Security
And the dandelions of suburbia.

As for the Emperor,
Even his enemies emulated his hairstyle.
A month of frost bought him an island.

This is all terribly bucolic, and that sort of thing,
But don't we deserve something more enlightening?
That's a rhetorical question.

Do me a favor and carry your firehose to someplace where it will be
    more useful, like a fire.

Instead of beating me over the head with it.

Always stay away from those
Who carry 'round a fire hose.

Solita Gauzeater and Jimmy Flagella
Were whiling away the time
Before their wedding
By screaming at each other.

They rode away in a chorus of tin cans.

A clean October day—
So clean you can see your reflection
In the dogwoods.

The act of dying is of no importance—it takes such a short time.

That house is in other hands now.
So is the town, for that matter.

WHATEVER WORKS

In the meantime, don't get too close to the guard dogs,
Especially the phosphorescent ones from the peat bog.

The inmates are wandering around my floor,
Standing there gossiping in front of my door.

The stake holding them looks a little stressed.
If they escape it can only be for the best.

I'm an ignoromnibus, it's true.
Would gladly pay you later for a few.

"What did you say?" he asked, grinning like an idiot.
These pants are a 38, they shouldn't fit.

Do you want an honest answer to that question?
You can multiply it by an obscure religious faction.

It lasted all day, whatever it was.
That was one way to get a buzz.

Time is both progressive and cyclical—
I was going places on my bicycle.

My shoelaces don't always cooperate.
And my pupils don't always dilate.

At least I don't have to report back to the talent agency
Regarding my level of plangency.

It takes more than a costume to become an actor,
You have to be up on the beauty factor.

His architecture aspires to invisibility.
His can openers are arranged in order of utility.

MANDATORY COMPULSION

The sharper the shaper the starker the stalker. As though some
Genius loci or all-seeing eye had suddenly got hold of me.

The eye was like a hurricane's, or the yoke of an egg.
Like a blind man in a clock shop you can hear the ticking

But you can't see the hands. You have no slide rule with which
To perform the altercations. I'm as much me as I can be.

If it's less you than you can be don't blame the admiralty.
The loyalty and usefulness of dogs, the beauty and grace

Of cats. There are two ways to destroy this debacle. Or rather to
Enjoy this tabernacle. The Pied Piper walking along the streets

Of Manhattan, humming a show tune, another "boffo number."
Or washing your hands a hundred times a day, and how it's like

Praying. Or how praying isn't so different from OCD, however
Sincerely it's meant to be. I should know. But the Lord knows

Best. Sad or glad, one size would fit all if we didn't need an
Infinite redress. The line of vision is always being interrupted

By the nosegay of desire. *I can see for miles and miles.* Where's
The fun in that, old man, in the interest of pulling your

Chain? The single, solitary dog who had the guts to bark at him
As the troops retreated. Meanwhile her ex-husband is survived by

His second wife, much to the discomfiture of her paramour
Or imprimatur. The bells and whistles would feel much better,

If only one could play them without the "tits and feathers."
A profound unmitigated loneliness is the only truth of life.

WOOLLY MAMMOTH

Eventually the permafrost surrendered him
To genetic speculation.

Gog and Magog, the door was agog.

Sort of goes without saying though.

Now I know I have to get
Myself out of trouble.

Before leaving town
Check the weather and your luggage.

Many words spoken to me have seemed English.

He instructed me in etiquette. Since when?

At certain times it seems more facile;
Those are the times to watch out for.

All attempts at eloquence
Are acts of seduction,
Most of which fail,

Just in case you didn't know.

Voices, for instance, of which there are so many saying so little.

Louder please, I can't hear you.

Or both at the same time?

But it's too late for that knowledge,
At least for the moment.

A fading Autumn day, back when I was so much simpler.

WHERE IS "AWAY?"

It's time to break out the castanets, the tambourines and bassoons.
It's time to dance around the willow tree.

"It's a little late for that," he said.

"Good thing I didn't contract lung cancer, I never would have lived it down."

The party people can't be blamed for their spontaneous combustion.
That's why someone has to be sure that the fire door isn't locked.

The sleep of a sheep, a sheepish sleep.
The sleep of a salamander, a sheepish salamander.
A skunk cabbage basking in its own swamp.

This is redolent of something—roasting meat for instance.

We go around and around the sun, but we grow old and die by the calendar.

I have forgotten all my Latin, every last declension. I keep a tiny
And completely useless bit stashed away in one of the distant corners of my
  brain.

The narcoleptic taxi driver, drifting peacefully through the red light.

The local FBI building has no windows, at least that a pedestrian can see.
It keeps out the dangerous gaze of people walking their dogs.

It might be too late, and it might be too early. It's hard to go on if you can't
  stand
The weather. Is it Naugahyde or leather, oil or acrylic, Vaseline or
  tambourines?

It may have an incredible kick, a "beautiful rush," business as usual.
But, like the working week, it will kill you if you keep messing around with it.

Or you could just throw them out. But where is out?

The news from elsewhere requires a warning label.
This maze must lead somewhere, or so theorized the rats in hell.

TRAP DOOR

Rods and reels, shovels and hoes, pitchforks and chandeliers,

The trap is the corrective, until you get the joke.

There was no place more beautiful than the garden from which we fell.

Which of these fruits and vegetables is juiciest?

Forensic motorboats churn the lake;

The world is spinning as in a blender.

I knew a software engineer who thought *per se* meant "for example."

There were summers when my garden was beautiful.

Even if we don't know when to laugh just yet.

With the mouth of a sailor.

There was no place more beautiful than the garden from which we fell.

We were sold, did what we were told, paid our money and took our choice.

The trap is the corrective, until you get the joke.

First thing we'll do, let's kill all the lawyers.

The tender trap, the bear trap, the Venus flytrap, the lobster trap.

There were summers when my garden was beautiful.

Forensic motorboats churn the lake.
I knew a software engineer who thought *per se* meant "for example."

What if he performed the joke and nobody attended?

UTILITY BELT

He worked hard to achieve a place from which.
> It didn't have class but it had utility.
"Taco Bell's Meningitis in B flat"— for which he stood corrected.
> *Life is a long lesson in humility.*

A hothouse tomato has no last resort.
> I'm lucky to have a two-foot square garden.
The FBI building, revisited, revealed the same tulips in the same place.
> My dreams of country life were never part of the bargain.

The elm seeds are thick on the branch and soon will be thick on the ground.
> It didn't have class but it had utility.
Only a few seeds of those thousands will produce new trees.
> *Life is a long lesson in humility.*

A fine head of cheese could be found at the monastery.
> I'm lucky to have a two-foot square garden.
Desire and ambition are counting machines.
> But my dreams of country life were never part of the bargain.

The 4 hottest fitness girls of the Instagram.
> It didn't have class but it had utility.
Always keep your head down, in the classroom and at the bar.
> *Life is a long lesson in humility.*

And does the mind solace itself in peevish sea gulls?
> I'm lucky to have a two-foot square garden.
The crossing guards were generally down and out—not good role models.
> My dreams of country life were never part of the bargain.

The girls were flummoxed by the boys and vice versa.
> It didn't have class but it had utility.
I've seen both ways of approaching the subject, and I didn't like either.
> *Life is a long lesson in humility.*

In the depths of the comfy chair was a random assortment of coins.
> I'm lucky to have a two-foot square garden.
Now I can buy me some beer.
> My dreams of country life were never part of the bargain.

HAZY ON THE DETAILS

When is it time
To spin a new bottle?

Every time I approach an inn,
There's suddenly no room.

Were you raised in a barn?

The downer horses
Make good glue.

Just over the hill,
They learned how shaggy it can get.

The working-class side of the hill,

Where the Kowalskis are.

And in the elevator
The woman with the hole in her throat
Coughing up bloody phlegm—

And still she smokes.

In the elevator with her,
I felt like getting sick.
Luckily, I was only going to the third floor.

[Insert apotropaic formulae here.]

So many bells
There's no telling
Where they're coming from.

It's how I know it's Sunday.

Oh, give me back
My sieve. And my wig.
Especially the wig.

And the sirens should shut up.
As should the gulls.

CATCHY TUNE

The music gets stuck in your head—
An infection, or infestation.

And the beat goes on,
At the mansion and the filling station.

The jack-o-lanterns of yesterday
Are the collapsed wrecks of tomorrow.

And lamb is a part of our reality,
With or without the mint jelly.

Then winter arrives.

There's not much to guess
And even less to know.

Let it snow, let it snow.

Forgive me if my concerns are mostly
For my own concern.

Why don't we do it in the road?
There's no easy answer, but someday you'll learn.

I pawned myself repeatedly,
But luckily, I was always able
To redeem myself.

Sometimes you feel like a prince
And sometimes like a toad.

Let them run, ride, strive
As so many fishes for a crumb,
Climb catch snatch, cozen—

I'll just sit here
Behind my drums,
Twiddling my thumbs.

FEASIBILITY STUDY

Normalcy and sanity
Were growing too far apart.

I got out of there by hook or crook.

Now I'm checking myself
To be sure my sanity
Is still about me.

"What's to fease?"

"The moon is high,"
He sang,
At the top of his lungs.

He was very hip guard.

"What's the feasibility
Of oats in Scotland?"

They accused me subtly
Of being under the delusion
That "it was all a dream."
But I went about my suffering anyway.

What did they know about it?
Maybe it was all a dream.

Or it could have been Memorex.

And there we stood,
Like a bunch of dwarves in evening wear,
Trying to round up the dressmaker.

Give me a big piece
Of something like that,
A wedge of lemon,
A slice of the pie,

When the moon is high.
This plate is crazed.
This duck is burnt,
This wine is corked.

Someone has been sleeping in my crib.

A well-worn watch
Knows the time.

The meeting was pointless anyway.

MANUFACTURING SECTOR

She did not ride on a donkey.
She did not wear buckles and bows.

She roared by without a muffler.
Then the windshield blew away.

It would have been
A difficult stile to get over anyway,
Especially on a donkey.

Doesn't everyone have a mortgage
On a big house at our age?

His wife worked for
The Ford Motor Company
Back in the day.

Are you developmentally impaired?

Wrong way go back.

And show us your driver's license.

"I believe in peace,"
Said the sales rep,
Extolling the virtues of the steering wheel
And its horns.

Don't burn your bridges until you're on the other side.

Don't burn your burgers on your gas grill.

America would be meaningless without cars.

REUNION

Just one more spin around the room.

It was just a stop on the tour.

Their stage smiles were an epiphenomenon or quirk.

"Remember me?"

"Where do you drink coffee these days?"

"Are you still in a band?"

"Are you the captain of the football team?"

Doo lang doo lang doo lang.

And at the museum
It doesn't pay
To look too hard at the center of things.

When was the last time you spent the day
Grinding maize in a stone pestle,
With a baby on your back?

But nothing has changed;

The show must go on.

DEAD BLUES

The game is fair play
But sometimes we run out of fun.

The fish are dead,
Long live the blues, or fish, as you will.

"It's just a game," they say.
Some games are more than we bargained for.

I shy away from games like a poorly trained horse.
A poorly trained horse shies away from me.

A poorly trained horse is shy.
And who can blame it

For hiding behind its mother's
Skirts, or skulking on the outskirts

Probably wearing a beard?
And the machines play on.

But I showed up anyway, dressed in blue.
Some games are more than we bargained for.

And now the hard-won blues were beginning
To stink. We caught more than we needed.

Skulking in corners, probably wearing a beard?
As for the machines how come they couldn't

Stick with rakes? They were a lot more fun,
And a lot quieter. Be fun, be gun. The guns have begun.

Actually, they've been gunning
For a long time. What or who in the world

Can make them stop? As I was blue and
The robots were here to stay, I declined to rsvp,

But I showed up anyway, dressed in blue.
Professor Slobberdash was not amused.

UNSPOKEN REGULATIONS

Like a pigeon, the seagull gobbles the Wonder bread, then wanders away.
What a strange duplication, what a weird thing to say.

Then the homeless man whose bread it was
Wanders through the tidal pools, sifting through the mud.

They were a match made in purgatory
Or nowhere—heaven shining above, hell steaming below.

Are we being punished for our sins?
Whatever I did I'll never do it again.

They wear their brains in their belly and their guts in their heads.
And now that their leader is king, it's the end.

The end of time, the end of peace—
So much for the poor in spirit and the least of these.

But bereavement happens in any case;
Even more than taxes, death can't be escaped.

"You're a rough customer" she said,
Implying I should have been either married or dead.

I was just waiting for the other shoe to fall,
Walking along, bouncing a green tennis ball.

The pregnant girl in the bake shop couldn't stop eating the cornbread.
The whole idea gave me a terrible sense of dread.

I was just waiting for the heavy ax to fall,
Wondering what they had against a green tennis ball.

A FLAW OF WIND

Somewhere between a hero and bored to death the blues stood
On the corner and lamented. The burnt-out boxer was boxed

Into a corner without his box cutter, trying to disentangle
The truth. He had enough ribbon to knit a bib.

Assailed by a flaw of wind, slapped about. Reef the jib,
Man the pinafore. Baby LeRoy and W.C. Fields walking down

The street hand in hand mumbling sweet nothings.
To be cryptic is to be in the dark, where the light don't shine.

Like a death threat overheard in casual conversation,
It was impossible to get the thread through the eye of the candle.

The life of an artist's model is one long tale of discomfort.
Let me give it to you straight, a right to the proboscis,

The rhinoceros. So much for the peaceable kingdom.
But an inferior mousetrap is better than

No mousetrap at all. Better than both is a cat. The dog
That's friend to man, the cat who's a rough customer.

She'll move heaven and earth to sit where she wants.
Our Lady of Sorrows cried us a river while the pipes

Of the happy organ boomed over the choir. Desire is endless
And then you die. The gargoyles gargling acid rain, the recorded

Church bells annoying us all over town. A happy organ indeed.
And how music never quite lives up to its promises.

A STEADY AND SINISTER SERENITY

Great fodder for fantasy when one was young.

Breaking into the front and carrying them out the back.

Fortunately, the astronauts landed on a dung heap and survived.

When she came away from the target, she left her silhouette in knives behind.

The structure kept getting higher regardless.

His pants were covered with paint. They were a panting.

The Astroturf was treated with flame retardant.

If God exists, I hope he has a good excuse.

Imagine a quarterback running a flaming football field.

Meanwhile, I was gritting my teeth, trying to force myself back to the fourth conjugation.

Hashish at the costume ball made it seem that much more like fall.

My mind keeps returning to the snappy retorts I didn't come up with.

The leader of the laundromat couldn't hold a torch to the coydogs.

Will it be a right boot or a left, a clodhopper or a Wellington?

There was no way around the fireplug.

IN HER DREAM

    ...that pause of space which I call "father"
Wasn't necessarily what he or anyone made him out to be.
    Still, she ran away. They wished she hadn't, because she mattered.
The secret of fathers is to make them what you want them to be.

    She was dressed in rags, bowing and dancing with a queen,
Who didn't smell so great herself, and had an unpleasant complexion.
    But despite the garlic breath, she was after all a queen.
Their tango took them in many directions.

    ...that pause of space which I call "father"
Was easily substituted with a mental image of the Duke.
    She ran away. They wished she hadn't, because she mattered.
At least she didn't leave everything behind—she took a book.

    She was dressed in rags, bowing and dancing with a queen,
This despite being "quite cured of seeking pleasure in society."
    And even with her royal garlic breath, the queen was after all a queen.
She was neither a card nor a chess piece, but the real deal.

    In the dream, *that pause of space which I call "father"*
Was very simply getting in everybody's way.
    She ran away. They wished she hadn't, because it mattered.
The dapper mannerist said it was "all part of being 'fey.'"

    She was dressed in rags, bowing and dancing with a queen.
Her father stood behind the starting gate, smoking a Pall Mall.
    But despite the queen's garlic breath, she was after all a queen.
They ran away, hand in hand, before the ash could fall.

    In the dream, *that pause of space which I call "father"*
Lent neither a hand nor $200 to his son the waif.
    The waif's girlfriend ran away. They wished she hadn't, because she mattered.
His father said, "They make it nice." He replied, "Don't underestimate the mess they make."

She was dressed in rags, bowing and dancing with a queen.
There's not much to say about something so outré.
But despite her garlic breath, the queen was still a queen.
Everything will be fine, as long we can keep the soldiers at bay.

CURRENT CONDITIONS

You seem more unusual than usual today.
You'd better straighten your tie if you want to stay.

I'm glad you think you know what you're doing.
Just watch out, the neighbors are suing.

Shallow or deep, life kills you in the end,
No matter how many kind cards you get.

A speech that was a model of the obvious:
It didn't take a genius to impress the lobbyist.

Don't spook the ghost, so to speak. And don't spook the moose.
Both of them are on the verge of breaking loose.

Have it when you can and accept it when you can't.
There's no use embarking on a supercilious rant.

It matters not how a man dies but how he lives.
You can't get anything if you have nothing to give.

The working day demands some sort of self-reclamation.
You need a lot of something to clean up the contamination.

Satisfied with kicking their seeds, the dandelions were okay by me.
And when in bloom I loved their smell—guttural and funky as aged
    cheese.

Elsewhere on the menu there's no end of crow to be consumed.
The diners and the crows were equally doomed.

If you can't afford to uphold your end of the bet
Bring your blunderbuss to the game, loaded with lead.

IS THIS A TEST?

The professor would have done anything
To acquire a babysitter, including lying and flattery.

Think about it though,
It must have had some humanistic value,
Some redeeming feature.

"Ilegitimi non carborundum;"
I will never be a classicist.

The dog ate my coupon book on the way to the store;
No patties for me today.

The overachiever considered cooking a waste of time
When he could be studying for the next exam.

I guess it depends on how much time you have.

How long will the borage last in storage?
What's the price of eggs in China?

"What is the role of plot in the postmodern novel?"

"Poverty makes men ridiculous."
But satisfaction brings them back.

What is the role of peanut butter in the postmodern brothel?

I can't get none. I try and I try.

It's a little discouraging
The way we are always looking
In the wrong direction.

But I'm sure I think about them
More than they think about me.

Let me reassure you,
The answer is at hand.

CRAWLING AROUND

Except for the beginning, everything went smoothly enough,
Until the end, which was more than a little rough.

Entropy makes a point of being there at all the wrong times.
The sirens in the background are only an excuse for the rhymes.

It didn't come in handy to have a pacific disposition.
The very bottom of the pile was my usual position.

Granted it gets a little boring most of the time.
That's why we need a few more glasses of wine.

But what happens to Kenny between episodes?
Do they harrow hell to resurrect his bones?

It's a telling question, and a rough road down which to crawl.
But after the sacrifice there's fresh milk for all.

Push it in on one side and it bulges out on the other.
Don't tell me things are getting better, brother.

Renting the garage was a luxury he couldn't afford;
He had to find a dirtier place to be bored.

Given enough pressure, any egg will crack,
And by then it will be too late to take it back.

Like a schoolyard bully he hated
The way I couldn't play the game.

He lost part of his face in the accident
But that side was never much to look at

Anyway. There's no hurry but you'd better hurry up.
Just ignore the corpses scattered in the dust.

STRANGE BREW

The politics of estrangement
Go galloping over the hill

Into the arms of Annie Oakley
Who puts down her gun briefly

To clean her glasses
In an estranged manner.

She's just like a dream
Of an old friend

Who looked like that,
But now is dead;
Who cleaned his "specs"
Just like that.

And with friends like that
Who needs enemies?

But mind your manners, stranger,
Or she'll give it to you, too,

For a few dollars more.
"For a nickel I will."

It's a witless outlier or outsider
Tied to ceramic insulators,
The new style in cement shoes.

If you tie on enough of them
They'll pull you down
Into the water and around the block.

Imagine drowning in a hurricane.

Or head-first in a toilet bowl.

The fish rots from the head.
Maybe there's something to be found,
Mainly there's something to be lost.

But the mutations don't care
If you find them or not,

Unlike the players,
Who prefer to be caught in the act.

FLUID SITUATION

In this best of all possible visions of hell
It's difficult to tell the water from the well.

It's difficult to tell the water anything. It refuses
To cooperate. Like chocolate from a vending machine,

The fat of the land was something I couldn't render.
That is, I couldn't render it realistically,

The schmaltz was gone. How about
Another waltz around the rink? Don't you think?

If I had the money I would buy the farm. As it is
I'm thrilled to be able barely to afford the barn.

Would it help if I wore a placard?
The poison ferns still looked lovely, waving

In the breeze. I think they're bracken. But it doesn't matter
What I think. To *go on from day to day, getting a little fatter.*

At some point it stopped making sense, or at any rate,
The sense it continued to make was irrelevant to its fate.

A sortie out of sorts discovered painting lakes.
That and turning sixty. I'm running out of birthday cake.

It takes a forklift to remove the bullshit coming down
The chute. We had a collective fit when we heard the news

Of all the socks that have been lost in action.
Just help me get the better of this contraption.

SILVER BULLET

Something noxious is knocking on the tip of my tongue.

I wonder who death thinks he is,
Coming around and spoiling all our fun.

Moist towelettes poised to clean up the mess.

The windsock had a predisposition to blow west.

Over what was left of the marshes the jumbo jet boomed.

Things never go as planned in love or war,
So take the battle plans and throw them on the floor.

If we could read the signs, we might know what's coming,
But they're illegible by design.

Every bullet has a silver lining, in theory at least.

He rose from his grave and took off running.

Things are never what we intend
When push comes to shove or worse to worst.

A wooden stake is a good thing to have on hand.

Gravity was an eccentric force,
Boiling the top down to its wobbly essence.

WANDERING DOWN

Take your time,
Take a letter, take it across town.

A letter framed in black,
Headed for the dead letter box.

Down in the valley it used to be better,
Cypress groves to wander about.

X marks the spot.

How's your credit and all that rot?

Part of me feels that it's too late.
But maybe it's always been too late.

The day has had lots of practice
At persisting 'til evening
When the shift changes.

Faced with extinction we did what we were told,
Or what we thought we were told.

It was difficult in the cold,
But waking we kept the candles lit.

And at the wake,
We ignored the warped relations,
For your information.

A tower of power, an observation tower.
The bread crumbs dropped, the picture cropped
So only the good parts show.

A FEATHER IN YOUR SKULL

Do me a shake and I'll tell you no lies.
What I want is a burger with fries.
I never had the dough. Would gladly pay

You yesterday. Don't worry about it.
When they were feeling flush, not trying
To fix the jakes, our fathers could be amusing.

Don't scuttle the boat till you can see the shore.
It would be a shame to drown,
Having left your stash hidden on the island.

The end is not in sight. We need plumbers' dope.
Actually, any kind of dope would be welcome at this point.
The inside dope, for instance. Or the outside.

Let's kick the gong around. But leave the plumber
To his work. He isn't paying much attention
To us anyway, except to insinuate his tip.

It must be a movement of the self itself
That brought us to this gallery.
And that's the way things get stuck in your head.

But it doesn't matter. Never mind.
Working a stupid job, they had roast beef
For lunch. I got tuna and was subsequently shamed.

Macaroni salad on wheat bread—
The soggiest sandwich you've ever seen.
"The streets are awash with it."

Can't you take a joke? Let me know when the big
Cheese comes of age; when the panther comes out
Of his cage; when the ballerina takes to the stage.

FALSE PRETENSES

I ask you to judge me by the enemies I have made.
There to see the show, she slid neatly onto the stool.
"Were you there?" "I was but I evaporated."
A good excuse for a life worth living without insurance.

Nothing has "genuine human appeal."
"I would have walked to Delaware."
It's a matter of what you like and whom you feel.
Where power lies, power lies.

I ask you to judge me by the enemies I have made.
But they were caught at the border.
"Were you there?" "I was but I evaporated."
One death of accumulated bile deserves another.

Nothing has "genuine human appeal."
Absolute power lies absolutely.
It's a matter of what you like and whom you feel.
Other times you're glad to get rid of it.

I ask you to judge me by the enemies I have made.
Strong enough to blow the man down.
"Were you there?" "I was but I evaporated."
As we stood at the door trying to decide.

Nothing has "genuine human appeal."
Making hay while the sun shines bright on my old Kentucky home.
It's a matter of what you like and whom you feel.
The correct form of OCD with which to appease the deity.

I ask you to judge me by the enemies I have made.
Eventually it gets easier to slam the door gently.
"Were you there?" "I was but I evaporated."
Her tortured imagery and my tortured syntax.

Nothing has "genuine human appeal."
In any case, they pull it off, or screw it up.
It's a matter of what you like and whom you feel.
And the living is easy. For someone else.

RUBBERNECKING

The unfortunate chicken wants to get back into its shell

And seal it up behind, with the last small bottle of Elmer's Glue it has left.

It will never make it across the road. They could at least stop

Throwing things at it. How do you feel? I feel like excoriating

The neighbors. Our mothers would have been scandalized.

Getting weepy is the key—the key of C.

But why should I care about the great perhaps? As for nostalgia, it's a toxin.

And who would want to watch that much TV anyway?

Don't shoot untill you see the whites of their eyes.

The brain has too many found objects on its mind;

Did anyone really say that, for instance, about "the whites of their eyes?"

I wasn't crazy about the mess, but I could usually find a table to myself.

And the weird sandwiches: peanut butter and lettuce on rye.

"Mad dogs on short leashes." Trust me, you don't want their slaver

Or palaver. I own that I cannot see as plainly as others do

Whatever it is everyone's gawking at. Too much carrion will spoil the fox.

HOT TAMALES

She monitors the floor
With her head around the door

While the stolen garden
Bakes in the patio sun.

And I sit here soaked in sweat
Waiting for the a/c filter to get dry.

But how the leftovers swarm!
It's a one-way street

From here on out.
And if the garden is stolen

Why should I water?
Swing your partner.

Dancing cheek to cheek.
It makes me want to go back to sleep.

Who was your source, the tap?
You don't miss water

Until you have to buy it in bottles.
Then you wake up and your kitchen is gone,

Replaced by a great hole
Gaping with rebar. "Annie get your gun."

And the potatoes are baking
In the potato sun. Never seen one?

Don't start searching now,
By this time they're way too hot to handle.

WHEEL OF FORTUNE

Sad in the city, sad in the country,
Heavy water in the arboretum.

A beautiful rush, business as usual.

The plaster cast of Rin-Tin-Tin
In your backyard
Has been sniffing something.

There's always something,
Or something more,
Slopping around out there.

You deserve a brick today—
Some smack in the head.
It was flying around in the storm.

And many failures.
But you were able to brush it off.

Paintings of wine labels, THC jelly beans; that nerve or chord

Continues reverberating with the in-crowd, which is almost
Everyone. We were trapped in time.
Take me out to the ball game.
We needed the sunglasses for medical reasons,
And they looked good.

But I'd rather see the world as it is,
Rain or shine, so to speak,
Including the thrilling bobble-head dolls.
Take me out to the ballgame,
Just don't leave me there, speaking of trapped.

Life moves forward
And around at the same time,
The earth around the sun,
The months making the same marks
In succeeding years,
The tire going around and around down the hill
To its rendezvous with the kerosene.
Does anyone have a match?

WATER WATER

There's a convention and a hotel to every purpose under heaven.

The stars look down on us with a grave sense of disappointment.

But that's not the worst of it.

Are you coming or not; don't make me wait forever.

The sky crying rain down the window or street.

Superimpose your reflection.

This glass is half empty.

I came down here for some purpose,
I just can't remember what it was.

My memory is a sign of the times.

I remember the tornado that came straight down from Niagara Falls,
As if in recompense.

Someone was killed by a falling tree. Windows were shattered.

A strange fluke for New England.

That was a long, long time ago.

Still, it was worth the wait.

UNDENIABLY

Typecast in the role he chose for and by himself,
He was always ready with a declamation.

But wherefore the panic, we wondered.

I have looked into it but I can't find
The gist at the bottom of the jar.

The till is empty.

Til then, goodnight.

This isn't an excuse or exercise.

I should say it's not *just* an excuse or exercise.

And if the best you can do is a letter,
Let it rip. Or rip it up. Or rip it off.

Did you get it? The part that is? The plot? The joke?

We can kick it down the road from here, or up the stairs.

Little triggers on your lips.

I got a word in edgewise.
And a pretty big word at that,
It barely fit.

And there it sat.

Me too.

The hooligans woke me with their yodeling.

I was craving something but I didn't know what.

Whatever it was it had nothing to do with you.

MARCH TIME

Try to remember the big storm.

God knows it's not by much. Maybe a hair.

It was you threw down the gauntlet.

The black cat crossed my path to get to the other side.

The various guises of the "regular guy."

Anxious as I was I triumphed on the stairs.

When we were in a fighting mood.

I played second fiddle in the school orchestra.

It's what I owe you for shooting the sheriff.

But I ain't superstitious.

What happens starts out from a long way off.

"What nice luggage you have grandma."

"All the better to visit you with my dear."

I was mean, you was mean, we was mean.

Just leave me to my own devices,

I've already failed all your dumb tests.

STATIC SILENCE

In slow motion with darling asides
The hounds on his tail in full cry.

Full beyond capacity with the dead
But all that malarkey is just in your head.

The joints have grown cold, the dinner postponed,
The time is all out of joint, that is to say deboned.

But don't worry outside is where I got me some hygiene.
I don't want to go there again but thank you very kindly.

Interference for the lie we'll learn by experience,
Like a T-shirt or button that says Low Clearance.

Depending on your base assumptions, vile creature,
Your every backward glance betrays your ugly features.

The holidays are already behind us and I barely noticed.
I guess they weren't much of an object for focus.

Is there any trash to be salvaged here,
Or any salvage to trash?

The conspiracy has given me pause
With which to greet the dawn

But I forgot to set my alarm.
Or else I slept right through it with my head on my arm.

The late-night drunken sailor ascending the stairs overhead—
It's impossible to assign him to the quick or the dead.

FREE-FLOATING ANXIETY

I stumbled into a hornet's nest
And then into a cow pie.
It wasn't my day, but it wasn't yours, either.

"Potato skins aren't food," he said,
"They belong in a pigsty."

Haven't you had deep-fried potato skins?

Bad weather always looks
Worse through a window.

You can beat me all you want,
I'll never be a believer.

But Mary knows best
How her garden grows.

"It's a nice day," Charlie said, "If you're a duck."
It was time to slop the pigs and pass the buck.

Military justice is to justice what military music is to music.

You don't need winter to develop a fever.
The disease showed up unexpectedly; be resourceful and use it.

The "horseless horseman,"
Whose meanings were meaningless,
Went far enough to discover certain secrets.

"Foods you never knew could make you beautiful"
Definitely aren't on the menu
At the next truck stop.

An infinite regress of useless tears

Welling in reaction to unnecessary fears.

DOES A BEAR?

The impulse to say anything about anything
Is as useless as singing

In the shower. I want to forget the blueberry metaphors forever;
All they do is depress the weather.

No amount of cleanser will remove the stain,
Even though everything else will go down the drain.

If it's been done it probably has to be done again.
Was it all the things you did or all the things you said?

Take a magazine to the bathroom. Take six;
Maybe if you read enough, you'll stop passing bricks.

And if you start out believing in original sin,
No amount of suction will clear up your skin.

Sex is overrated. Or maybe I should say over-determined.
Good sex for me is bad sex for Herman.

Who's Herman? Someone who walked in
Off the street, where the original occupant had been.

Does a fish swim in the woods? Does a bear retch in the car?
Eat what you kill and don't go out too far.

The wind itself is a vocation.
What did you do on your summer vacation?

The fact is industry and love of truth alone won't win Olive Oyl
Anymore. Buy her a big diamond, while waiting for the spinach to boil.

STRIPTEASE

I've had breakfast but I'm still hungry.

My sea legs are still at sea.

Coffee is the reality principle.

I'll have to be famous by myself; I have been in the gutter.

The boss said, "Look what the cat dragged in."

But it was the best I could do—why fake it?

Nevertheless, I will continue with the funk.

How can people who are so smart be so dumb?

The body is another self; its priorities are slightly different.

Speak louder—when was the last time you took a shower?

Sex is the enemy of reason,

That's why it's easier for the young.

In my dream, the ghost of Peppermint Patty

Wanted to perform for the soldiers.

TRUE NORTH

The abstracted pedestrian was busy nursing his sciatica
At the crosswalks, the worse for wear. And his little dog too.

But he went about his suffering anyway,

And business as usual.
Was he ill? With a perpetual complaint?
And in which doctor's province did it fall?

Which is to say someone beyond all other remedies,
For whom there is no remedy.

Our province is the plain;
Oh give me a home.

On the other hand,
"Said Tweedle Dum to Tweedle Dee…"
And he was right.

I am very fond of my rattle
And of the mysterious noises
Made by the plumbing.

But Halloween is not what it used to be.
Remember those wax teeth we used to get,
That had something like Kool-Aid in them?
Pretty disgusting actually,
But they seemed like fun at the time.

And at the clothes or boundary line, it was hard to get orientated.
She used to like standing with her arms out,
Pretending she was a compass needle.

It was cute,
But it never helped us find our way home.

RESPONSORY

      It's a hierarchy, complete with hierarchs.
Low on the roster, Popeye is in the rigging,
      Who never had the pleasure of a spinach salad.
And the cat can sleep for hours, twitching.

      Forgive me my transgressions
As reported in crumbling comic books, ripe with dew.
      Cleverness for its own sake is a defense against feeling things directly.
Whether or not we were introduced, we had no idea who Tim was.

      It's a hierarchy, complete with hierarchs.
They pace themselves by watching each other work.
      Who never had the pleasure of a spinach salad.
The Italian gardener said Dante Alighieri was a "big cheese."

      Forgive me my transgressions, Tim.
Are you here to stay or just visiting?
      Cleverness for its own sake is a defense against feeling things directly.
Tim was someone who was with the general at the time.

      It's a hierarchy, complete with hierarchs.
Not to mention matriarchs and patriarchs.
      Who never had the pleasure of a spinach salad.
But it's a realm in which I don't belong.

      Forgive me my transgressions.
Sometimes discovering the obvious hurts.
      Cleverness for its own sake is a defense against feeling things directly,
For example. I was out of old material so I had to think on my feet.

      It's a hierarchy, complete with hierarchs.
And I should know. And Superman,
      Who never had the pleasure of a spinach salad.
My chestnuts were too hairy this year, along with my ears.

      Forgive me my transgressions.
We made much of it, as comedy of the absurd.
      Cleverness for its own sake is a defense against feeling things directly.
Time goes forward and around simultaneously.

TWENTY MULES

Once broken halt, damaged lame.

It's your own resistance.

The muse wants to make everything melodic,

But there's more than one way to skin a lion.

The rain in New Haven falls mainly on the pavement.

Getting away is a good place for you.

She breathes for the ghost of us, sometimes in disguise.

Your noise to spite his face *(sic)*.

I'll have to make a lot of it.

They were all a syllable or 16th note behind,

So there's this out-of-synch vibration,

Like a rattling washing machine.

But if it tastes good eat it—the big man's fallacy.

Can we take a detour around this mess?

It bores me. Trapped in a classy red convertible

That doesn't run, or a rusty black pickup that does.

WHITE NOISE

Looking at you looking at me, save your breath.
Don't raise a flap or go away mad, just leave.
With a rock tied to his leg he came up to breathe
One last time, torn up, tickled to death,

As though there were anything funny about it. Time
Was a sing-along anyway, something to beat
Until it was dead, something to treat
Of. Something is broken in this state of mind

And no watch repair shop can repair it.
"Death's a reformer," of the most reliable kind.
"Make a line, form a line, in line, out of line."
Priapus god of gardens guarding the top of the stairs.

"Here I sit, broken hearted;" should such poetry get
Into poetry? What am I, some kind of creep?
The usual thimble of soda isn't too deep,
Just dig. But call the gas company first, or don't let

On you broke the main. And stop blushing,
You aren't that good of an actor. How weary
The theorists grow, trying to fill the void with theories.
We are our own top predator, our own competitor. A rushing

Sound, a horrid stench, were signs of the harpies coming for us,
Their beaks and talons honed to a keen edge.
The clangor of their wings terrified the man on the ledge.
It was his job to keep the corner turning, the buses

Turning the corner of third and third in morning traffic.
Thank goodness for a good pair of legs. On some immortal
Or immoral day he spun the dial and found a portal
To another dimension where the atmosphere is mostly static.

AGGRESSIVE INGRATES

"Take good care." As opposed to what, "bad care?"

The little traps laid for us by the world,
The danger of falling glass.

Some were playing cards and some were shooting craps.

Something I could have lived without couldn't live without me.

I envy the wrecking ball, replete with rubble.

The state of my digestive system is always making trouble.

Every dog has his due provided she's sufficiently serious.
Unless they're attack dogs, rabid dogs, fight dogs . . .

Deleterious was a bad habit with Sirius.

The 250 year old barn still stands up to the rain.

Look, an ant, get out the antibiotics!

Here comes a candle to light you to bed.

I'm so hungry I could eat a wedding cake.
But where would I start? With the figurines?

A useful jar to put things in, a set of Tupperware in delft.

How infernal do you want your curry?

"It's almost like you don't care."

THE INCREDIBLE SHRINKING MAN

I'm an ignoromnibus, it's true.
Would gladly pay you later for a few.

We've heard it all before;
The only thing we want is more.

A word to the wise is incised
On your hairy forearm. But you're alive

Which is more than some of us could say.

Scouring the landscape for loose change,
The light got in her eyes.
Or was it smoke?

In any case, we're never far from the original joke.
That's what you get for being broke.

And speaking of smoke,
I remember having a chemistry set
And giving it everything I could get.

Nowadays I'm obsessed with coffee beans
And whiskey bottles,
Just more of the same.

Won't you step into my parlor
Said a spider to a fly.
Afterwards the fly sported a ghastly pallor,

Hung out to dry.

This is the best part of the trip!
Which doesn't matter, with a black eye and lip.

By now, the movie is a little juvenile,
Unless you're high.
The spider's still scary though.

Reversion to a tiny size,
We are what we used to be,
At least sometimes.

STUPID QUESTION

The horseman with his head under his arm stood on one
Side of the starting gate and I on the other. Maybe it was fun,

But we couldn't get over it. "Keep your chin up," he said,
As his chin sagged to the floor. He was better off dead.

It will be what it will be, said my best friend tautologically;
If you're really that fed-up you can always go to sea.

The uncertainty principle in a worried place,
Are there any lessons to communicate?

That is, any truths that aren't negated by other truths?
Narcissism was the name of the game. Her middle name was Ruth.

There is such a thing as a stupid question, that's what keeps
Them in business. You sow, you reap, you get it. "That's deep."

The girls work together, getting the formulae
Of girlhood down. The boys like to be mean, and that's no lie.

It's not even an exaggeration. But I don't want those sorts
Of friendships no more. "At the food court

You could meet your future wife." Which I didn't want to do.
If it was up to her all men would be either married or neutered.

Luckily for us, it ain't. There's a limit to the number
Of fingers one can lose to this huge threshing machine that hums

Along like a superconductor or a pedal steel guitar.
If you're looking for trouble you don't have to look very far.

CHANCE ENCOUNTER

As with cotton stuck in the neck of a medicine bottle,
I couldn't get a grip. But nobody was counting.

Let's put you in charge of hunting down
Whatever hasn't been captured yet.

The principles of romance are close enough.

"May she continue to rest in peace."

All this makes cherries. It even makes no more.

"Famous last words," as we used to say.

There's no law that it should be done
But there's no law against doing it.

Once you do it though, you'd better run.

The ship's hold was full of lollipops—
The many child stars were in their element.

It will never happen that way again.

I just want to take the whole pile of rubbish
And throw it up in the air,
High enough for the wind to catch it
And carry it to Siberia where they need it
Like a hole in the head.

We're in deep shit—the fire is coming closer.

Get out your water pistol,
Get out your slingshot.

In other words,
A snowball in hell.

But someone else was there first.
They planted a flag.

ACCIDENTAL DISASTER

Indispensable figments of my imagination.

Becky beckons.

Whichever direction I go it's the wrong way.

She was a nurse
With a sexy voice
And nothing to say.

What does it mean to have lost one's sneakers in a dream?

Old high school yearbooks don't amount to much.

What kind of a guy
Are you and I?

Despite all his faults he really was an idiot.

A vice when successful is called virtue.

In my father's high school yearbook:
"From a drip to a dope."

Pictures of an exhibitionist.

A blow with a word strikes deeper than a blow with a sword.

I got cars you got cars all god's children got cars.

Distracted by his neurosis,
He forgot to change the oil.

THE APPLE OF DISCORD

Accounts of the fall of Paris were burned in the streets of Troy, New York.
    This had me worried for a while, then I took a deep breath.
Release the hounds thereof, man the ramparts.
    Look back in anger, look back in shame.

A lesson in getting nowhere fast, without getting caught.
    In general, no one can see the dark side of the moon.
The behavior you started out faking has become part of your personality.
    Let's get together again sometime soon.

And the metal numbers on telephone poles.
    This had me worried for a while, then I took a deeper breath.
Heave away my hearties, row row your boats.
    Look back in anger, look back in shame.

What a good boy am I,
    In general. No one can see the dark side of the moon.
We do things because we must, not because we want to.
    Let's get together again sometime soon.

And whatever you do, don't take your lay in coats, or quotes.
    This had me worried for a while, then I took a deep breath.
Something utterly trivial and of ultimate importance ruined my day.
    Look back in anger, look back in shame.

Can I switch name tags with you rich?
    In general, no one can see the dark side of the moon.
I know it's a terrible thing to ask.
    Let's get together again sometime soon.

Sometimes the best direction is to find the way out.
    This had me worried for a while, then I took a deeper breath.
Yessir, Mr. GI Bill, get out the Uzis.
    Look back in anger, look back in shame.

The windows continue absorbing your inflection.
	In general, no one can see the dark side of the moon (except the scientists).
Falling Glass Next Ten Miles.
		Let's get together again sometime soon.

HIGH NOON

A nervous breakdown on paper, a lot to think about in the hospital.

The skein over which the funambulists funambulated.

I had to look it up three or four times.

A medley, an edible arrangement.

John Lennon playing the tuba.

Who you or he might be in somebody else's reverie is beyond me.

Start by getting a lot of paint on the canvas.

He was a likely candidate for spontaneous combustion.

Post mortem, a small pile of greasy ashes.

Our eyes and other senses will commonly deceive us.

There were so many doohickeys it was hard to tell them apart.

Release the hounds.

And the eagles of the great republic laugh, ha ha.

I broke the circular sander.

In the bathroom when he was feeling flush.

Is it what they buy or what they earn?

Mr. Krook burst into flame.

Getting and spending we lay waste our powers.

Something else to get stuck in your head.

I broke the circular sander.

But satisfaction brought it back.

A nervous breakdown on paper, a lot to think about in the hospital.

THE BIRDS

The rubble accumulates,
Along with the pigeon pies.

Or perhaps they are a form of sadness,
Like the boxes of Red Hots we bought
At the comic book store.

No one wants to know
What made them hot.

But their packages disappear
With the first rain, giving themselves up.

And death shall have no dominion.

The tangle of languages that language was,

While in the topiary the birds
Are speaking a language from which we are
Permanently excluded.

As for me, I'm convinced some sort
Of communication is going on,
Even if it's only rhythmic.

But perhaps they're just lying in wait,
Like in the Hitchcock movie:
The lovebirds want to love us to death.

Don't look now—some kid with a slingshot is after
The sparrows again. And I remember
A dream about "a demon pig named Jodie;"

It brought me to this impasse.

A single isolated cell in the corporate
Petri dish with bars behind which strippers
Make a good buck. And to run by the river gilded

With sun and birdsong on any green morning
No longer with embossed place settings got
The names of the guests all wrong.

STUDY GROUP

Just when I thought it was getting good it began to suck.
I was going to bring you a load of quotes but they took away my truck.

The forbidden fruit in the flesh never quite lives up to the intensity of our desire.
Beware the prestidigitation of the scholars and the illusions of the buyers.

Don't over-quote the overcoat; find out what it's really worth.
Making a silk purse from a sow's ear is as plausible as the virgin birth.

Up on the roof an empty Bacardi bottle marked the ledge.
Someone was probably considering a landing in the hedge.

"The level of discourse was disappointing," which was an easy way of baling out.
My malarkey wasn't up to the standards of the intellectual boy scouts.

Did you think this running commentary was some kind of impractical joke?
If your anxiety gets any worse the performance will make you choke.

Maybe he brought it on himself. But of whom might that not be said?
I should write a book to find out if there's anything in my head.

The man in the frame had a lot of brains but not much imagination.
His feelings of impatience trumped his feelings of elucidation.

But never mind about his blue period, which of his periods wasn't?
When you're doing pastry, they're better by the dozen.

If it's relief I'm finding here, it's a double-edged sword.
But even though we're high strung, at least we're not bored.

WAITING ROOM

The only way is through.
At the moment it seems impossible:

No thoroughfare.
I mean how do you trust yourself?

And your neurotransmitters?

And those are just a few of many
Things to worry about.

Why wake up in the morning?

There must be something that makes it worthwhile.

There must be something
To fix or shrink.

But I've never seen a shrink
Who didn't make me worse.

Most of them needed me more
Than I needed them,

Like the one with no waiting room.

(You had to wait on the porch—that didn't last long.)

And there's something to drink
On the top shelf.

"Not the cause, just the symptoms."

You want to know about my mother?
I'll tell you about my mother!

Watch out for charged particles,
They can be very aggressive.

This page is intentionally left blank,
And the one behind it
Is unintelligible.

HAUNTING AND HUNTING

Will this be like the FBI building? A crisis
Just across the street? Can I get there on foot?
It's only a block away. More important,
What will I wear? More of the same no doubt.
They say that this one and that one wears this
And that. I don't. You would need a lot of cats

And keep them hungry. They like
A good granary. They had a lot of wheat
In ancient Egypt. And garlic. That's a lot of
Rodents. "That always makes it nice."
Do they still make hay? While the sun shines?
"Depends on who your boyfriend is."

All in the interests of reportage. Most of the people
That I get worked up about are dead. But
They live on in my head. The only difference
Between me and a mad person is that
I'm not mad. The only difference between me
And a fool is that I'm nobody's fool.

"If that's the way you want to spend your Sunday…"
The upward movement of birds, especially crows.
It was somewhere in-between
Snow-boarding and an ancient
Sled race or buffalo hunt. The huskies
Were champing at the bit.

Although I don't think they use bits.
They might not even use huskies.
As soon as a woman was present
He had to begin seducing her.
Except that there probably won't be a next time.—
Too much water under the bridge.

A danger of drowning was averted.
There are better ways to spend your Sundays.
Weight-lifting for instance. Or snow-boarding.
But the cat came back, in caps and cap guns.
She was beautiful in a cowboy hat
But it was too late to get on board for that.

GENERAL DRIFT

As we drift deeper into the dark we can see for miles and miles.

The world not as we perceive it
But as it is does not exist.
He had a Hail Mary and a Holy Ghost.

How sadly departing strikes us
And where it strikes us we now know.

But he was part of
The big machine, the machine in which
I was never really interested.

"It's important to be an omnivore in this life."
I used to agree to agree, now I'm not so sure.

The kaleidoscope got narrower as he turned it,
Like a form of tunnel vision or stricture.

How casually people wound each other,
Usually completely unconsciously.

Do you know where your children are?

"How could you not know?"

A vaudeville Theseus getting tangled in Ariadne's thread.

Sometimes the sanest reaction
To insanity is the aspiration to invisibility.

Reading comic books is one way to make the afternoon disappear
When you should be out networking with your playmates.

Handing out gum to the dance class at year's end,
When it had been prohibited all year,
He thought he was showing profound charm.
He was lucky nobody choked.

But it was enough to know that the Canon Aspirin was around—
Row row your boat.

How strange the cigarette boat
Looked from the shore.

Do you think it will get us there in time?

With neither confession nor extreme unction?
A deathbed conversion, just in case.

But these are conversational extremes,
Anti-social misconstructions.

ACKNOWLEDGMENTS

Grateful acknowledgment is made to the journals in which many of the poems in this book first appeared:

Poetry Pacific: "Unspoken Regulations," "The Other Hand"

Rasputin: "Accidental Disaster," "The Usual Miscalculations," "Offerings"

Bending Genres: "Ambient Emergencies"

AMP: "Keeping Busy"

Unlikely Stories: "Mandatory Compulsion"

Otoliths: "In Her Dream," "Wandering Down," "The Apple of Discord," "The Apples"

Offcourse: "Trap Door," "Catchy Tune," "Reunion," "A Steady & Sinister Serenity," "Current Conditions," "Hot Tamales," "Wheel of Fortune"

Meniscus: "Is This a Test?"

Dash: "Fluid Situation"

Muddy River Poetry Review: "Silver Bullet"

First Literary Review-East: "Water Water"

The Halcyone: "20 Mules"

Blazevox: "Free-Floating Anxiety," "Chance Encounter," "Aggressive Ingrates," "Static Silence," "True North"

Twisted Vine: "Responsory"

Panoply: "The Birds"

Manhattanville Review: "A Flaw of Wind"

Oddball Magazine: "Hazy on the Details"

Isacoustics: "Where is 'Away,'" "Board Meeting"

American Journal of Poetry: "Helicon," "Utility Belt"

Visitant: "Woolly Mammoth"

Home Planet News: "By This Time," "Strange Brew," "Dead Blues"

The Big Windows Review: "Whatever Works"

By This Time is **Ian Ganassi**'s third poetry collection. Ian is a retired dance accompanist, having played African and Caribbean percussion for dance classes for at least 30 years. As a poet and musician he has collaborated with dancers and musicians throughout the New York metropolitan area. Since 2005 he has collaborated with the painter Laura Bell on an ongoing collage project called The Corpses (after the surrealist parlor game). The collages have appeared in galleries, literary journals, and other venues. The Corpses now have gallery representation with Jennifer Baahng Gallery. The covers of all three of Ian's books are collages from the series. He has published poetry in numerous literary journals, including *The Yale Review, The American Journal of Poetry, New American Writing* and *Blazevox*, among many others. His two other collections are *Mean Numbers* and *True for the Moment*.

www.ingramcontent.com/pod-product-compliance
Lightning Source LLC
Chambersburg PA
CBHW020338170426
43200CB00006B/434